The Widow's Journal

Questions to Guide You through Grief and Life Planning after the Loss of a Partner

The Widow's Journal

**Questions to Guide You through Grief and
Life Planning after the Loss of a Partner**

Carrie P. Freeman, PhD

CreateSpace
Charleston, SC, USA
www.thewidowsjournal.com

See the website for the book at www.thewidowsjournal.com

Printed by CreateSpace, an Amazon.com company
Charleston, SC USA

Cover Design by CreateSpace. Cover floral background art credited to Torky, and the bird art to Embra from Thinkstockphotos.com. Author portrait by annpackwoodphotography.com. Interior Design by artist Katie Welch (cmykatie.com). The drawings purchased from Dreamstime.com are: Torky's "abstract floral seamless pattern" used on the chapter title pages, and Torky also drew the "floral bird" (who has the floral pattern within him), and Kitekit's "hand-drawn vintage decorative elements" for the flourishes and some leaves. The drawings purchased from Thinkstockphotos. com are: the cute finch looking down, who is the same bird featured on the cover and on most pages, credited to Embra from "two birds;" as are all the flowers used throughout, from Embra's "set of abstract flowers;" and Embra also drew the little finch who is looking back over her shoulder at us, taken from Embra's "floral seamless background."

ISBN: 1515193314
ISBN 13: 9781515193319
Library of Congress Control Number: 2015912078
CreateSpace Independent Publishing Platform, North Charleston, SC

Contents

Chapter One
INTRODUCTION

I was widowed right before my thirtieth birthday, in 2001, just a few weeks after September 11th. I was married to a loving guy, Dave, who died during a stem-cell transplant at age thirty-one during his second bout with cancer—he first had bone cancer, followed by leukemia. We met in a kung fu class and were together in Florida for six years (married for two of them), and our only kids were cats.

While I was mourning, I used every resource and tactic I could to help me cope: books, individual therapy, group therapy through hospice, friends, meditation and yoga, time in nature, exercise, uplifting music, funny movies, nutritious food, baths, tea, dark chocolate, and eventually antidepressants. I recommend you do it all; whatever it takes to help you. It takes a lot.

I also used journaling as a form of personal therapy and still do more than a dozen years later. The good thing about writing your thoughts in a journal is the privacy it offers – you can be completely candid with no one to judge you, and no one for you to bore, because you can choose to go over tedious or repetitious thoughts as many times as you want or need to. With a journal, you are free to express just how bad you *really* feel, without worrying your friends, family, and coworkers.

However, the point of this book is not just to purge but to progress. *The Widow's Journal: Questions to Guide You through Grief and Life Planning after the Loss of a Partner* is your comforting space for personal therapy and expression. It's also a guided planning process—a sanctuary for you to determine what you really care about, what you want, how you can bounce back to experience joy again, and what you should do to make your life meaningful in this new and unexpected chapter after losing your life partner. Unlike many books on grief, *The Widow's Journal* doesn't tell you what you should do or feel, and it isn't a memoir or collection of other people's stories. Instead, similar to a workbook, it asks you relevant, frank, and provoking questions so you can better clarify and understand what you are feeling. Sometimes it lets you wallow, but primarily it asks you how you can better cope and take care of yourself, how you want to interact with others (including potentially dating again), how you want to commemorate your loved one, how you want to live your new life, how you can find meaning and purpose by helping others, what you regret, and what you appreciate.

Throughout the book,
I refer to your late partner by using the phrase
"your loved one."

While I am writing from the perspective of a young American female who lost my husband, I designed this journal with the hope that it would be useful to anyone of any age, gender, or sexual orientation who lost a romantic life partner, although it probably leans toward the viewpoint of a woman with a long life ahead. To be open to everyone, whether religious or not, this book does not assume any particular faith and approaches the bereavement process from a secular standpoint, allowing you to incorporate any spirituality into your answers in your own way. Additionally, you may have children, perhaps kids living at home, and being widowed has made you a single parent. While this book focuses on you as a person rather than you as a parent, you will naturally weave those family concerns into your answers. An advantage to concentrating on your individual identity and your own self-care, as this book privileges, is that you will have more to give as a parent.

I have grouped approximately 100 questions into chapters categorized from earlier to later periods of grief (from right after you are widowed to months and several years later). It might make sense to answer the questions somewhat in order, but it's also OK to jump to any set of questions that move you. I recommend including a date on every entry so you can assess your development over time. I preface each chapter with some context for what kinds of questions I address in this chapter and why. You'll also often see my comments in italics above each set of questions to give you some insight into why I think those questions are useful or how they relate to my own experience. The final chapters are designed for you to gather your most poignant observations and inspirations to create tangible affirmations and images that can guide you. If you feel like you need affirmation statements and inspirational images sooner in the grieving process, then start working on them in the back of the book at any time, adding on to them as you progress through the earlier chapters of the book. Consider writing in a beautiful color with a pen you like the feel of. This journal should be a comfort to you.

You should be hopeful that you will survive this and eventually thrive again. When I was first in mourning, I felt like the rug had been pulled out from under me, and I was floating unanchored, grasping to find stability and meaning to ground my life again. When Dave died, I was working in human resources, conducting leadership training and professional development classes, but we had made plans that I would go to graduate school to become a professor. In fact, I had to postpone the start of my studies to be his caretaker after we learned he needed a stem-cell transplant. To fulfill my career goal after he passed, I went on to get a master's degree from the University of Georgia and then a doctoral degree in communication from the University of Oregon; I have been teaching and publishing scholarly research at Georgia State University in Atlanta since 2008, earning tenure and a promotion to Associate Professor of Communication in 2014. Outside of my career, another thing that makes life meaningful for me—besides watching comedy programming—has been my volunteer work in the animal protection movement for several decades; I currently co-host animal and environmental protection radio shows and write about animal advocacy. I live in Atlanta with my rescued dog, Elliott, near my parents and my brother, his wife, and their kids and dog. I still stay in touch with Dave's family. They live in South Africa, including a young nephew named in his honor. I have managed to build a foundation again to feel more grounded and content in my life, and I hope this book lets you see that you can do the same in your life.

I have set out here to write the kind of bereavement book that I could have used when I was first widowed. As a teacher and a former workshop designer, I appreciate personalized exercises and guiding questions that help me uncover truths and plan my future. Even though your bereavement situation is likely unique to mine in many ways, I think you will find the process of answering these questions highly useful and a valuable complement to the therapeutic guidance you should be getting from professional grief counseling. I picture you keeping this journal in your bedside table and taking it out each night or morning to spend some quality time focusing on yourself and your recovery. Any time you spend on taking care of yourself is time well spent.

Chapter Two
EARLIEST STAGES OF GRIEF

*F*or this first section I focus on core questions that are basic yet big, as you and your friends and family are orienting yourself to the shock of your loved one's passing. I ask social-oriented questions about how you will respond to others, how you want them to respond to you, and how you will ask for the help you will naturally need from your support network. There are philosophical questions about beliefs on death, the way the world should work, and what your loved one would want for you or would feel if situations were reversed. There are also therapeutic questions prompting you to plan for commemorating your loved one and saying anything that was left unsaid.

I encourage you to let friends and family know what you need. They really do want to help you but probably don't know how. Sometimes, if friends don't know how to help and therefore feel uncomfortable, they might end up leaving you alone after the funeral, which probably isn't what you want.

What do you want your friends and family to do for you during this trying time? What would be helpful? What do you expect or think is an appropriate response from them?

What do you pledge to do for other friends who experience grief?

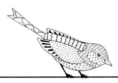

When people ask you, "How are you doing?" the normal response to that common question is "Good," or "OK," but that's probably not the case for you now.

What do you want to say when people ask you how you are doing?

How could you explain that succinctly to them?

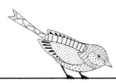

Are you having trouble getting past *the way* your loved one died?

Is there someone you need to forgive, including any misguided guilt you may feel yourself?

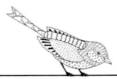

To put things in perspective, it can be a helpful thought-exercise to ask hypothetical questions about what your loved one would be doing if your situations were reversed and it was he/she grieving for you. If your loved one could talk to you now, he/she would likely want you to be happy again and not suffer for long. Can you be that merciful to yourself?

What do you think your loved one would be doing if it had been you who had died instead?

What would you want your loved one to feel or do if the positions were reversed?

What do you think your loved one's future would have been without you?

If he/she could talk to you now, what advice do you think your loved one would offer you about your future and what he/she wants for you?

Taking care of yourself should be your top priority in the first several years after your partner's death.

To what extent are you taking care of yourself and making that a priority?

Does that feel selfish, or is it simply wise and self-sustaining?

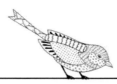

What could you do for yourself to take care of yourself and feel better:

Each day?   Each week?   Each month?

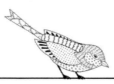

What principle, advice, or religious teaching can you draw upon that is most helpful and comforting to you?

How can you remind yourself of this guiding concept every day?

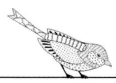

Do you feel worse for your loved one because he/she died and missed the opportunity for a longer life, or do you feel worse for yourself for having to live without your loved one?

Is the grief mainly for *yourself* and the future you have lost?

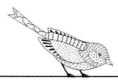

I remember feeling so deflated thinking that I now had to adjust to a life that wasn't going to be as good as it once was. That's a hard belief to reconcile with. Either I could accept it or I could hope that it wasn't true, as how could I know what life had in store for me? Your story is still being written.

A question you may dread facing is, do you think the best years of your life are behind you?

You can't be sure, but what if they might be? What are your new expectations for the next phases in your life?

Since you know how painful grief is, you certainly don't want to put your loved ones through losing you. It's important to realize that you won't feel this level of pain forever and seek the immediate help of a licensed therapist if you experience suicidal thoughts or feelings of hopelessness (I refer to these myself as "unproductive thoughts"). The loss of a life partner is so debilitating to one's sense of self and stability that it is only natural that all of us need professional grief counseling to recover.

A hard question to consider is, if your thoughts become so negative that you start to feel that life is not worth living anymore, how will you save yourself?

Where is the line, or what is the sign, that you feel you can't cope productively and need urgent intervention from friends and professional counselors?

Who would you tell, or how do you promise yourself you'll get help to get through this lowest phase?

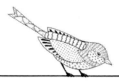

It would be nice to feel there is a tangible legacy for your loved one (in addition to any children). It could be something you plan to do in the future and slowly save for, so as not to deprive yourself in the first few years when you are adjusting to a new (and often reduced) income level.

What kind of event or permanent commemoration would be most befitting of your loved one's interests, traits, and personality?

Determine which of these options you can afford or will need to start raising funds to achieve.

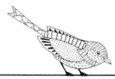

Losing a spouse really rocks your foundation and causes you to question your views on life, death, justice, and how the world works in your attempts to come to terms with why this happened to you.

Do you think everything happens for a reason and this was fated, or do you think this was random and just unfortunate, as death is a natural part of life and happens every day to countless living beings?

Why should you be the exception?

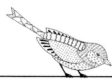

Why do horrible people like murderers sometimes live long lives, and then good people like productive citizens and loving partners die prematurely?

How does this unfairness test your faith (either your religious faith or your faith in the way the world is supposed to work)?

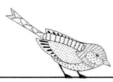

What would you like to tell your loved one if you had the chance? Was there anything left unsaid? Say it out loud now in addition to writing it down.

Chapter Three
EARLY TO MIDDLE STAGES OF GRIEF

*T*his chapter is for after the initial funeral and memorials are over, the sympathy cards have stopped arriving, the attention lessens, and you are trying to adapt to a new normal. Questions at this stage assess how well you are coping and what could further aid your healing. You'll also need to decide how much to talk about your loved one with close friends and family and whether to mention your loved one at all to new acquaintances. I've included some pragmatic questions about financial and career planning as well as some deeper, more inspirational questions about making your life meaningful, determining what virtues you most want to live by, and reframing your situation from one of loss of life to gratitude for a precious relationship.

One way to show self-care and hopefulness is to evaluate your own progress and check in with others to get their feedback on how you are doing.

What makes you proud of the way you are coping?

Where is there room for improvement?

What ideas do you (or professionals) have to help yourself improve?

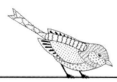

Does feeling bad make you feel good in some way? How?

When do you anticipate the acute pain will diminish? What would it take for that to happen for you?

Envision and describe a time when you believe you'll feel like yourself again and experience contentment. Practice feeling that way now.

Do you feel better at a certain time of day? (Morning? Afternoon? Night? Any time it is mealtime?)

What location makes you feel loneliest?

What location makes you feel better? Would it help to go there more often?

In this time when you are reassessing your own self-identity and figuring out what is most important in life, consider how virtue ethics can help in that process of character building. The Ancient Greek philosophers didn't ask what was the right thing to do or the right outcome but rather, what was the right kind of person to be, believing that the rest would fall into place based on developing good character. They focused on living according to key virtues like honesty, loyalty, generosity, humor, fairness, compassion, temperance, and courage.

Which of your loved one's virtues do you most want to emulate as a tribute?

How will you exhibit this trait in your life?

Which current virtues of your own do you not want to lose as part of your identity?

How can you develop these virtues and further express them in your life?

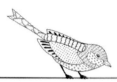

For me to be hopeful about life and my future in a time when I was feeling so depressed, I had to reassess what makes life fulfilling, and how I could live a more meaningful life.

What makes life meaningful for you?

How has the meaning of life changed through the years for you?

Do you see things differently now after being widowed? How has it changed your view on living a meaningful life?

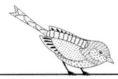

One of the many good things about journaling is that you can use it to imagine new realities and create or live out fantasies that give you some joy. These can be about your loved one or they can be about anything you want for your life.

What fantasies or dreams do you have?

Does thinking about these dreams soothe and entertain you, or is it counterproductive?

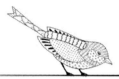

Losing your partner presents pragmatic financial concerns that can add to your burden. Spend some time brainstorming solutions to meet your needs and gain some financial stability.

What concerns about money do you have in terms of changes to your family income?

What is your new monthly budget to pay your bills, and how can you make it work?

If necessary, what are some options for bringing in additional income?

How can you ensure you are taking care of your retirement income needs?

In the earliest stages of grief, almost everyone in your circle knew of your loss and you didn't have to explain it. As time goes on, you start to encounter new people who don't know your history and you have to decide how much to share, when, and with whom. For example, it's hard to seamlessly work the topic of a loved one's death into a conversation while you are socializing, but it can also be hard to tell stories about your life without mentioning your partner or the fact that you were married. I had to make decisions constantly about when I was willing to mention my "late husband," cueing people in to the fact that I was widowed. Would I stop the flow of the conversation and talk about his death in more detail, as there is natural curiosity, or just let the conversation proceed on its original course? I find that if I bring up my late husband at all, I am more apt to mention him in social situations rather than work-related situations.

How will you bring up your loved one's death to new acquaintances, colleagues, or friends? And when? Under what circumstances is it warranted to mention?

How much detail do you feel you should give them?

How can you keep it from being a downer or making other people feel too uncomfortable talking about it—or feel they aren't supposed to talk about anything else after you drop that bombshell?

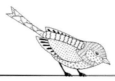

Your closer friends and family may look to you (or maybe you wish they would) to know how much to talk about your loved one in daily life.

Do you want your friends and family to talk about your loved one? How often, or in what way?

How can you clue them in to what types of discussions are welcomed and therapeutic?

If your family members say something that might be hurtful to you but was meant as a compliment to your love one, such as "You're never going to meet someone that good again," how do you feel you should respond?

I wanted my friends and family to know that even though I was naturally depressed, they could still count on me as a friend (to some degree), so I tried to show them that it's OK for them to talk about their problems too, however trivial. For example, if they told me their boss annoyed them at work, I didn't want to shut them down by saying, "Oh, yeah? Well, at least the love of your life isn't dead." I felt like this humility was a way of me being more approachable and staying in their lives (avoiding isolation), as well as feeling a bit more normal myself. I didn't want them to feel they had to treat me so gingerly like I'm made of glass and all we can talk about is my despair.

How much do you have to give as a friend to others in terms of being willing not just to share your own troubles but also to listen to theirs? Is it too soon for that?

What can you do to indicate to your loved ones that their problems also matter, however minor they may be?

Making long-term goals, like for your career, can be a sign of hopefulness, and it also helps you plan your financial future. For me, it was motivating to experience the change of pace of moving away, going to graduate school, and being stimulated by learning and carving out a new career path.

What are your personal career goals for where you want to be and what you want to be doing:

In one year?

In three years?

In five years?

In fifteen years?

My sister-in-law told me that grief was something you had to go through and couldn't go around. I found that was profound advice, and it was encouraging to know that by allowing myself to grieve, despite the pain, I was actually progressing and healing. But the goal is to eventually feel better and to be excited about life again. Make those plans for yourself.

What are your mental health goals for who you want to be and how you want to feel:

In one year?

In three years?

In five years?

In fifteen years?

You may not have known when you first fell in love that you would outlive your loved one. We must appreciate the time we have with our favorite people, as life is uncertain and short. It is a temporary privilege. Your time with your loved one was a gift.

While you feel that you lost your loved one, is it helpful to reconceive of your relationship and say that ultimately you were fortunate to have met in time to know, love, and be loved by him/her?

Chapter Four
MIDDLE STAGES OF GRIEF

*A*s the months pass you may be dismayed to realize you are still suffering, and perhaps more so than you were right after your loved one died. I found that to be true for myself. Adjusting to the reality of a daily routine without Dave was hard to bear and I was not getting as much attention from friends anymore, as they were back to their normal routines too. It felt very lonely. So, a few questions in this chapter do acknowledge the deep pain, how to deal with it, how you want to handle birthdays and anniversaries, and what happiness means to you. But a lot of the questions in this chapter are about planning for your new life, including writing a mission statement, doing charitable work, and considering dating again. I also include some provocative questions that ask you to consider any advantages in your new situation, what you have to be grateful for, and what you might do differently in hindsight.

The calendar has so many dates that remind you of significant events and milestones in your relationship. You can choose to celebrate them, mourn them, or perhaps even ignore them. For myself, I liked to make small symbolic gestures on significant days (looking at pictures, lighting candles, writing in my journal, etc.), but I didn't allow myself to get overly sentimental and more despondent on those days. I found that I missed him just as much on a normal Monday as I did on our anniversary. This may be different from your experience.

How do you feel about anniversaries and your loved one's birthday?

Which do you think should be commemorated by you, and how? Or is it counterproductive to overemphasize the meaning of certain days?

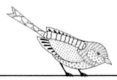

If you had a happy, committed relationship, you may look forward to having one again as a way to live a fulfilling life. I did. So, when a male friend told me that he would be hesitant to date a widow because he would be afraid he might never live up to the memory of her husband, he didn't realize how discouraged that made me feel about my own prospects. Someone who has lost a partner probably doesn't want to hear they are not likely to find one again. You hope that people will avoid making assumptions about you forever living in the past when they hear you were widowed. In reality, I have found that if you are open to new relationships, many people will be open to you.

Are you afraid others will view you as damaged, fragile, or forever hung up on the loss of your late-partner, especially at your job or when you are dating?

If you wish to, how can you convey a certain kind of inner strength and openness to new relationships or new challenges?

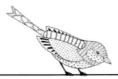

Sometimes I remember wanting to escape my own body because I didn't have anywhere to go for relief from the pain in my chest and an overwhelming feeling of sorrow. I would usually go sit at the beach at sunset or go for a walk, hoping the beautiful scenery would offer some reprieve. Spending time with a close friend, including my cat, would sometimes help. Going to sleep at night was sometimes my only relief, as I tended to feel better in the mornings.

What do you think can help when the pain seems overwhelming and you can't escape its physical and emotional weight? What are some of the best ideas from your therapist?

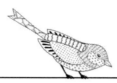

For me, thinking of how I could help others was one way to find purpose in my life. Since I saw how heartbreaking illness, death, and loss could be, I found it therapeutic to find ways to help others avoid that suffering and save lives.

If life now seems more precious, how can you enhance the lives of others?

How can you save or extend the lives of others, including nonhuman life like animals, trees, and ecosystems?

Married or single, kids or no kids, lots of different life situations have their pros and cons. No one can have it all. I might at times envy the affection and energy of my friends' family life with kids and they might at times envy my freedom to travel overseas for work. You are used to thinking in terms of what you have lost, but is there anything, however slight, that you have gained? The privacy of your journal allows you to candidly answer a delicate question like this.

What about being single is an advantage, liberating, or pleasant?

What won't you miss about being with your loved one, even if you feel guilty admitting it?

What do you think your loved one would guess that you would say here, like if you were a contestant on The Newlywed Game? Compare this to your secret answer that you wouldn't want to have admitted to him/her.

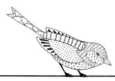

Mission statements are not just for organizations; they are also useful for us as individuals to clarify our values, goals, and priorities, offering a guiding focus to keep us on track and to serve as inspiration. As you likely feel your life's plan was yanked out from under you when your loved one died, it can be important to design a new foundation for your life.

Why do you believe you were placed here (wherever you are), with all your talents, at this point in human history?

Does living without your loved one change the mission, purpose, and direction of your life? In what way?

What is your mission statement? If you don't have a mission statement yet, consider creating one now. Try to keep it simple at just a few sentences that can guide each day and express what you stand for, what you want from life, and what you hope to achieve and leave as a legacy.

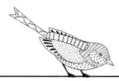

This is another question that has you reframe your situation from one of focusing on loss to focusing on what you gained. Gratitude can be a powerful healing force that, when felt deeply, crowds out sadness.

Now that you have lived without your loved one for a while, what have you recognized that he/she added to your life that can be a source of gratitude for you?

Sometimes when I'm sad, I wallow in it and wish for happiness. Other times, I find it helpful to blow it off by saying "So what if I'm sad? Why do I need to focus so much on my personal happiness when there are all kinds of other more important things (and so much more acute sadness) to address in the world?" Taking this 'universal' viewpoint can either serve to make you feel small and insignificant or it can instill a sense of humility that helps put things in perspective so you can concentrate on experiencing other emotions and goals besides just personal happiness.

What does being happy mean to you?

How important is your personal happiness? Is it overrated?
If so, what emotions should rank higher as a priority?

How does it change your view to put your happiness within a universal perspective compared to other issues in the world?

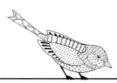

This is a rather profound hypothetical question about regret and if you would do anything differently if you could go back in time; it's ideal to explore within the privacy of your personal journal.

In hindsight, since you have been enduring such grief, was it the right decision to be with your loved one, even though you've ended up alone right now?

Was it worth the heartbreak you are experiencing?

If you could go back in time and do something differently, like remain single or pick someone else to date or marry, would you?

Does everything meaningful have to last a lifetime to be worthwhile?

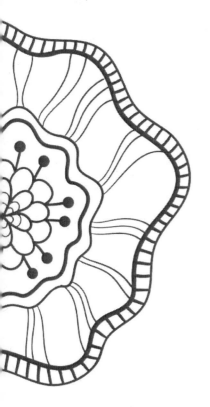

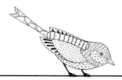

I always knew that I wanted to get married again and would eventually start dating, and even though I profoundly missed my husband, I was encouraged by the dream of having another loving partner someday. It's hard to know when or if you should start dating again, and there are lots of social pressures put on widows based on society's expectations of what mourning should look like and how long it should last. But whether you wait a long time or start experimenting with dating sooner, remember that when your partner is deceased, there is no such thing as cheating on him/her. It's your decision. Just be mindful if you are dating for the right reasons and being protective enough of yourself, recognizing whether dating is helpful to your recovery process or not at this point.

When is it OK in your mind to start dating again? How will you know?

How does that compare with what society or your social circle thinks? Who decides—you or them?

Who have you noticed that you find attractive? What impulses and desires do you feel?

Are you ashamed to admit them or act upon them? Why?

How will being alone or a sexual martyr help? What will it really prove?

Chapter Five
LATER STAGES OF GRIEF

*T*his last section of journaling questions is for after the first year of your mourning process. Personally, I didn't start feeling better until the third year, and that was with the help of antidepressant medication (although, you may not need medication at all or you may choose to start sooner than I did, depending on what your therapist thinks). How long your more acute stages of grief lasts depends on a lot of factors, such as the suddenness and circumstances of the death, how long you and your loved one had been together, whether you had kids, and whether you have found a new partner. In this chapter, I keep the questions simple but meaningful – reflecting on what you have learned about grief and romantic relationships, your new identity as an independent person, how and if gratitude can lead to contentment, and how you can make the most of the years you have left.

We are all going to die. We just don't know exactly when. Having seen your loved one pass emphasizes how fragile and precious life is and encourages us to make the most of the time we ourselves have left. But what does the notion of "living life to its fullest" mean to you?

How would you live your life and use your time if you knew when you were going to die?

How would having a time frame for your longevity change your lifestyle:

    If you might pass any day now?

    If you only had a year to live?

    If you only had about five years to live?

    If you had another decade or two, max?

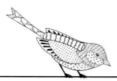

Contemplate your new identity as a single person and not as your loved one's significant other. You could describe yourself as "independent" if you think it sounds more affirmative than "single," but I like to recognize that humans are all dependent on others in many ways, whether single or coupled (and we are all interdependent beings ecologically).

Now that you and your loved one are no longer a couple, how does that change how you (or others) see yourself?

What have you discovered about your own identity and who you are as a person?

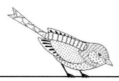

If you are dating again, consider what you now know you need or deserve in a partner to be happy and fulfilled in a relationship. I think it is much preferred to remain single/independent rather than settle for a mediocre or dysfunctional relationship. But it is worth taking the risk of loving again if you find another very special person well suited to you who could be your new best friend and life partner.

What traits do you want to look for in a romantic partner?

What have you learned about love and relationships that will benefit you in a new partnership?

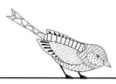

Buddhists describe nirvana as a state of contentment and peace of mind reached by ceasing to long for anything more and finding grace and gratitude in what you have.

List all the things you are grateful for. Consider keeping a daily gratitude journal.

Is nirvana possible for you now? Or would that just be lying to yourself and settling?

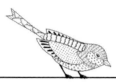

You probably didn't want to learn the lesson of how to grieve and recover from a heartbreaking loss. But you have gained new insights that could help others who will inevitably suffer their own losses.

Looking back in this journal and reflecting on your answers and your journey through grief, what advice would you give someone who just lost their romantic partner?

Chapter Six

GREATEST INSIGHTS

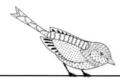

Look back and reread your answers in this journal. Feel free to add new comments to those sections (in a new color and with the date) to show how some of your views have changed over time. Collect your most poignant and insightful observations, and write them in this section as a summary.

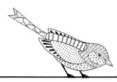

Consider your life's mission. Write your personal mission statement here.

List the top virtues you most want to live by. Consider ranking them and explaining how you can embody them in daily life.

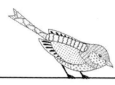

List the ways you will take care of yourself and make your recovery a priority.

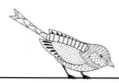

List ways that you will take care of others and enhance their lives.

Chapter Seven

AFFIRMATIONS

This chapter builds on the last and takes your insights and goals and has you rewrite them as "affirmations" that you can use for daily inspiration to help ensure your thoughts are productive and positive.

Rewrite some of your insights as concise affirmations that reinforce what you believe about yourself, your mission, and your future. Write them in the first person (for example: "I am...") and in a positive sense ("I appreciate my many fortunes" rather than "I don't take things for granted"). Carefully choose each word so it conveys the most direct, active, and animated action while still maintaining your authentic voice.

You may want to write them in pencil first and then come back after a few days and edit them. Then list them in this section, composing them in your best handwriting with your favorite color ink.

Write each affirmation on a note card and post them where you will see them each day: at home inside the front door, on a bedside table, or over the sink; in the car or on your bike; in your wallet; or in your desk or locker at work. Have reminder affirmations texted to yourself periodically. The important thing is to read them out loud to yourself each day, as the repetition will serve to reinforce their truths in your mind over time.

You have been in the daily routine of feeling low over the past months or years, and you may have been in the habit of crying daily. Now start to make feeling good a physical habit for your mind and body. Do so by using these affirmation statements as morning meditations, concentrating on how positive they make you feel. Carry that feeling throughout your day.

Chapter Eight
PHOTO GALLERY

There are some things words cannot express. And those things go here.

Inspiration
On these pages, post images that inspire you and help you appreciatc life. These photos may be expressive in some way of your affirmations.

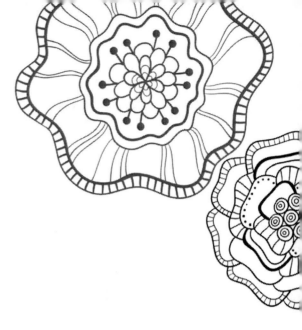

Gratitude

On these pages, post your favorite photo of you and your loved one, and write a statement of gratitude for the time you spent together and the fact that you met. Surround this picture with photos of other important people who are currently in your life—your best friends (companion animals included) and most supportive family members.

Humor

On these pages, post photos of images that make you laugh—or would, in theory, if you weren't so depressed right now.

Beauty

On these pages, post photos of images that you find beautiful.
It's perfectly acceptable to include some pictures of yourself here.

Aspirations

On these pages, post photos of anyone or anything (including relationships, jobs, and companion animals) that you want to bring into your life or places that you want to visit or live in the future. While you are grateful for what you currently have, it's fun to have new things to look forward to in your ever-changing life.

**Luxuriate often
in the last few sections of this journal
(your photos, insights, and affirmations).**

**Taking care of yourself is time well spent.
It will get you where you deserve to be.**